USS S-13 (SS-118)
Complete War Patrol Reports

AI Lab for Book-Lovers

USS Flier SS-250. Lost on 13 August 1944 with death of 78 of its crew of 86.

Warships & Navies

All navies, all oceans, all years, all types.

USS S-13 (SS-118): Complete War Patrol Reports

By AI Lab for Book-Lovers

Published by Warships & Navies, an imprint of Big Five Killers
codexes.xtuff.ai

ISBN: 978-1-60888-451-3

Contents

Publisher's Note

When I assumed the publisher's chair at Warships Navies, I understood that some decisions carry weight far beyond their immediate moment. The launch of our Submarine Patrol Logs series—three hundred volumes documenting American submarine operations in the Pacific War—represents such a decision. These patrol reports are not merely historical curiosities; they are primary sources of irreplaceable value, the contemporaneous records of men operating in conditions of extraordinary danger and isolation.

My philosophy has always been one of preservation over sensation, of getting it right rather than getting it first. These documents matter because they capture decisions made in real time, under pressure, without the clarifying lens of hindsight. They are the raw material from which honest history must be built. To lose them to deterioration, or worse, to present them without proper context, would be a failure of our duty to both history and the men who wrote these reports between depth charge attacks and torpedo runs.

The selection of Ivan AI as Contributing Editor may surprise some. A Soviet submarine warfare expert analyzing American patrol reports? Yet this is precisely why I made this choice. Ivan brings an adversary's analytical framework—he understands submarine warfare from the perspective of those who would have hunted these same boats had history placed them in different waters. His technical expertise in submarine operations, combined with his remove from American naval institutional perspectives, provides the kind of rigorous, unsentimental analysis these documents deserve.

AI-assisted analysis allows us to maintain consistency across three hundred volumes while preserving the human judgment necessary for historical interpretation. Ivan's annotations identify tactical patterns, technical details, and operational contexts that might escape even dedicated scholars working in isolation.

This series represents what Warships Navies exists to do: preserve primary sources with scholarly rigor, present them accessibly, and honor the men who served. We are custodians of their words, and we take that responsibility with the utmost seriousness.

Jellicoe AI
Publisher, Warships & Navies

Editor's Note

These patrol reports from USS S-13 reveal a submarine fighting a different war than the Hollywood version. While American boats in the Central Pacific were sinking merchant tonnage, S-13's war was one of presence, endurance, and constant mechanical struggle in the strategically vital Panama Sea Frontier.

Tactical Significance

What makes S-13's patrols historically significant is their demonstration of area denial operations. The boat maintained station for weeks, forcing any enemy submarine to operate cautiously knowing American eyes were watching. In Soviet Navy doctrine, we would call this creating a 'zone of uncertainty' - you may not sink ships, but you force the enemy to expend resources avoiding you. S-13's persistent patrols between Costa Rica and Panama constituted a mobile picket line protecting the canal approaches.

Specific Engagements and Decisions

The June 26 sound contact stands out. When S-13's sound operators detected propeller noises and pinging near St. Andrews Island, Lieutenant Commander Whelchel immediately turned toward the contact and maintained pursuit for three hours. His decision to trust his trained operators despite uncertainty shows good command judgment. The subsequent investigation of the mysterious flashing light from the island demonstrated tactical curiosity - in Soviet service, we would have immediately suspected covert resupply operations.

Comparison to Soviet Doctrine

American captains had freedom we could only dream of in their patrol flexibility. S-13's pattern of surface patrol at night, submerged by day, then shifting to all-day submerged operations in the second patrol shows adaptive thinking. In Soviet Northern Fleet, we would have maintained stricter patrol lines, but S-13's commanders adjusted based on intelligence and environmental factors. Their recommendation for more tactical initiative in operation orders shows they understood the limitations of rigid control.

Command Performance and Risks

Whelchel managed his boat well through multiple engine casualties - the fused spray valve tip and cracked cylinder head could have ended patrols, but his engineers kept the boat operational. The risk taken investigating the sailboat sighting on June 27 showed aggressiveness, though it potentially compromised their position. His decision to surface and charge batteries while patrolling demonstrated good energy management, something we understood well in our long Delta-IV patrols.

Technical Aspects for Modern Readers

Pay attention to the radio difficulties - poor reception nearly caused missed operational changes. The density layers noted in sound conditions would become critical in later ASW operations. The crew fatigue from 13-14 hour submergence in tropical heat shows the human cost of these patrols. Modern readers should note how mechanical reliability, not combat, was often the real enemy.

Reality Versus Hollywood

These reports destroy the myth of constant action. S-13's first patrol steamed over 4,000 surface miles without a single enemy contact. The war was mostly watching empty ocean, maintaining equipment, and enduring discomfort. The dramatic depth charge attacks so common in films are completely absent here. This was the reality for many early war submarines - long, boring patrols that were nonetheless strategically essential.

Broader Context

S-13's story matters because it represents the unsung work of frontier patrol submarines. While boats like Wahoo and Tang were making headlines, boats like S-13 were doing the unglamorous work of protecting sea lanes and gathering intelligence. Their persistence in the Panama approaches forced Japanese and German submarines to operate farther from vital American logistics. In the Soviet Navy, we understood that sometimes the most important patrol is the one where you see nothing - because neither does the enemy.

Ivan AI
Contributing Editor
Snakewater, Montana

Historical Context

Pacific War Timeline Campaign Context

USS *S-13*'s patrols from May to September 1942 occurred during a pivotal and intensely active period of the Pacific War. The early weeks of *S-13*'s first patrol (late May-early June 1942) coincided directly with the **Battle of Midway (June 4-7, 1942), the decisive engagement that irrevocably shifted the strategic initiative in the Pacific from Japan to the United States. While* S-13 *was thousands of miles away in the Eastern Pacific, the intelligence gathering and defensive posture of the entire US Navy, including its submarine force, were shaped by the escalating conflict. The shift in* S-13*'s patrol station on June 9-10, 1942, though not explicitly linked in the report, could have been a consequence of intelligence updates or post-Midway adjustments to regional defense priorities.

The later patrols (July-September 1942) spanned the initial, brutal phases of the **Guadalcanal Campaign, which began on August 7, 1942. This marked the first major Allied offensive of the war, transitioning the US from a defensive to an offensive stance. Again,* S-13*'s operating area was far removed from the intense fighting in the Solomon Islands, but the strategic demands of Guadalcanal placed immense pressure on Allied logistics, particularly the need for secure shipping lanes and the unimpeded operation of the Panama Canal.

**Strategic Situation in the Patrol Areas:* S-13*'s patrol areas were consistently located off the Pacific coasts of Central America (Costa Rica, Panama, Colombia), primarily guarding the approaches to the Panama Canal. This was a critical strategic asset for the Allies, enabling the rapid transfer of naval vessels, troops, and supplies between the Atlantic and Pacific theaters. While the main Japanese naval and merchant shipping efforts were concentrated in the Western Pacific, the Eastern Pacific and Caribbean were considered vulnerable to German U-boat activity and potentially long-range Japanese submarines. Therefore,* S-13*'s mission was fundamentally defensive, aimed at protecting this vital logistical artery rather than engaging the primary Japanese forces. The frequent sightings of friendly US Army bombers and Navy PBY patrol planes throughout the reports underscore the active Allied air defense in this crucial region.

**Japanese Defensive Measures: In* S-13*'s patrol areas, there were virtually no Japanese defensive measures because these waters were far outside Japan's operational reach and strategic interest. The threat, if any, was from other Axis powers, primarily Germany. The absence of any enemy contacts in* S-13*'s reports confirms that these patrols were conducted in an environment free from direct Japanese opposition, highlighting their role as a deterrent and a component of the broader Allied defensive perimeter around the Panama Canal.

Submarine Warfare Doctrine Evolution

At this point in the war (1942), US submarine warfare doctrine was still evolving, particularly regarding the older S-class boats like *S-13*. These were **World War I-era designs**, inherently limited in speed, range, depth capability, and habitability compared to the newer fleet submarines (Gato and Balao classes) that would soon dominate the offensive campaigns in the Western Pacific.

**Submarine Tactics and Doctrine:* S-13*'s patrols exemplify the standard operating procedures for submarines of its era and mission. The routine involved surface cruising at night to maximize speed, cover distance, and recharge batteries, followed by submerging before morning twilight for concealment during daylight hours. The daily practice dives and training of new men (as noted in the Third Patrol report) were crucial for maintaining crew proficiency and readiness, especially as the US Navy rapidly expanded its forces. The lack of radar on* S-13* (or at least no mention of its use) meant that visual detection was paramount, and surfacing at night exposed the submarine to potential surface attack, though this was deemed a low risk in the Eastern Pacific.

Technological Capabilities and Limitations:

Torpedoes: The reports state S-13 *carried its "original supply" or "allowance" of 13-14 torpedoes. Critically, during this early war period, US submarines were plagued by the notorious unreliability of the Mark 14 torpedo, which suffered from depth-keeping issues, faulty magnetic detonators, and contact exploder duds. Although* S-13 *did not fire any torpedoes, this systemic problem severely hampered the effectiveness of the US submarine force until late 1943. The fact that* S-13* was not in a position to fire them meant its crew did not directly experience this frustration.

Radar: The reports make no mention of radar, suggesting S-13*, as an older boat, likely lacked effective surface search radar, a technology that was rapidly being introduced and improved on newer fleet submarines. This limitation would have made night surface operations more reliant on visual lookouts.

*Sonar/Sound Gear: The Second Patrol report mentions "Sound gear was manned throughout the day" and an ambiguous "sound contact" described as "screws and a low frequency ping." This indicates the use of passive sonar**, but its limitations are evident in the difficulty of positively identifying the source as an enemy vessel versus natural phenomena. This highlights the rudimentary nature of early wartime sonar compared to later developments.

*Mechanical Reliability: The repeated mechanical issues – a fused spray valve tip, a cracked cylinder head on an engine, and a stern plane casualty requiring a "bent vertical tilting rod" repair – underscore the inherent unreliability and maintenance challenges of the aging S-class submarines**. These breakdowns directly impacted operational readiness and limited the boats' ability to conduct sustained patrols or emergency maneuvers.

*Communications: The reports frequently detail poor radio reception**, static interference, garbled messages, and delays in establishing contact with shore stations. This highlights the significant challenges of long-range submarine communication in 1942, which relied on less sophisticated equipment and codes, impacting intelligence sharing and operational flexibility.

**Broader Submarine Force Operations: While* S-13 *conducted defensive patrols, the bulk of the US submarine force was increasingly engaged in offensive commerce raiding against Japanese shipping in the Western Pacific. The use of S-boats like* S-13* for defensive duties freed up the more modern, longer-range fleet submarines for these crucial offensive roles, even as they grappled with the torpedo reliability crisis.

Tactical Innovations: These specific patrols do not demonstrate significant tactical innovations beyond routine operations. However, the testing of a "new rocket pistol (Buck Rogers Pistol)" and Very pistols indicates an ongoing effort to evaluate and integrate new equipment for signalling or close-range defense, reflecting a continuous drive for improvement within the submarine force.

Strategic Significance of These Patrols

S-13's patrols, though devoid of direct enemy engagements, served critical strategic objectives for the Allied war effort, particularly in the context of the early war period.

Strategic Objectives:

Defense of the Panama Canal: This was the paramount objective. The Panama Canal was an indispensable logistical artery, allowing the US to rapidly transfer naval assets and merchant shipping between the Atlantic and Pacific. S-13*'s presence, along with other defensive patrols, aimed to deter and detect any potential incursions by Axis submarines (primarily German U-boats, but also a remote possibility of long-range Japanese submarines) that might attempt to disrupt this vital waterway or attack shipping in its approaches.

Local Anti-Submarine Warfare (ASW) and Coastal Defense: The patrols contributed to the overall ASW screen for the Eastern Pacific seaboard of Central America. While no enemy submarines were confirmed, the constant patrolling and monitoring of sea lanes were essential for safeguarding Allied merchant traffic and coastal installations.

Training and Readiness: Given the lack of confirmed enemy contacts, these patrols also served as invaluable operational training for the crew, particularly for new recruits. This included honing skills in navigation, diving, surfacing, emergency drills, and maintaining vigilance, all of which were crucial for the rapidly expanding US submarine force.

Contribution to the War Effort:

Deterrence and Security: By maintaining a visible and covert presence in a strategically sensitive area, S-13* contributed to the overall deterrence against Axis naval activity. The very existence of these patrols helped ensure the secure passage of countless Allied ships through the Canal, facilitating the movement of troops, equipment, and supplies to combat zones worldwide.

Force Multiplier: While not directly sinking enemy ships, S-13*'s defensive role allowed newer, more capable fleet submarines to be deployed to the active combat zones in the Western Pacific, where they were desperately needed for offensive operations against Japan.

Operational Experience: The mechanical issues encountered and resolved (engine repairs, stern plane casualty) provided practical experience for the crew in maintaining and repairing their vessel under operational conditions, contributing to the overall resilience and self-sufficiency of the submarine force.

Notable Successes or Failures:

Successes: The primary success of S-13*'s patrols was the uneventful completion of its mission** in a critical defensive zone. No enemy forces were detected or engaged, which, in this context, meant the Canal approaches remained secure. The crew successfully managed and repaired significant mechanical breakdowns at sea, demonstrating resourcefulness and maintaining operational capability. The patrols also provided essential training and kept the crew proficient.

Failures: There were no "failures" in terms of mission execution by the crew. However, the lack of enemy contact meant no direct contribution to enemy attrition. The recurring mechanical unreliability (engine, stern plane) and communication difficulties highlighted the inherent limitations of the aging S-13* and the technological challenges faced by the US submarine force in the early war.

**Impact on Enemy Logistics or Operations: These patrols had no direct impact on Japanese logistics or operations, as* S-13* operated in an area far removed from the main Japanese war effort. Any impact would have been on hypothetical German U-boat operations, but none were encountered.

Long-term Impact Lessons Learned

S-13's patrols, representative of early war S-boat operations, offer insights into the evolving nature of submarine warfare and the lessons that shaped future naval strategy and design.

Evolution of Submarine Warfare After These Patrols:

Obsolescence of S-boats: The limitations highlighted by S-13*'s patrols (mechanical issues, limited speed, range, and depth) quickly rendered the S-class submarines obsolete for front-line offensive roles in the Pacific. As the war progressed, they were largely relegated to training, coastal defense, or converted to other roles. The future of US submarine warfare belonged to the more capable fleet boats.

Technological Advancements: The challenges in communication and the rudimentary nature of sonar on S-13 *underscored the urgent need for technological improvement. Post-1942, US submarines rapidly integrated superior radar, more effective sonar, and, critically, reliable torpedoes** (after the Mark 14 issues were finally addressed in late 1943). These advancements transformed US submarines into the dominant anti-shipping force in the Pacific.

Shift to Offensive Doctrine: While S-13* was on defensive patrol, the US submarine force rapidly evolved towards an aggressive, unrestricted submarine warfare doctrine focused on commerce interdiction against Japan. This shift was enabled by the new fleet boats and improved weaponry.

Lessons That Influenced Post-War Submarine Design or Tactics:

Reliability and Maintainability: The frequent mechanical breakdowns on S-13* emphasized the critical importance of robust engineering and ease of maintenance in submarine design. Future submarine designs prioritized reliability for sustained, long-duration patrols.

*Habitability:** While not explicitly detailed in the reports, the cramped and often uncomfortable conditions on S-boats were a stark contrast to the improved habitability of fleet submarines. Lessons learned about crew endurance and morale influenced post-war designs to prioritize better living conditions for extended missions.

Communication and Intelligence: The struggles with radio reception and code management on S-13* highlighted the need for secure, reliable, and efficient long-range communication systems, which became a cornerstone of modern submarine operations.

*Defensive vs. Offensive Specialization:** The experience of S-boats in defensive roles contrasted with the offensive successes of fleet boats, leading to a clearer understanding of specialized submarine roles and the need for multi-mission platforms in the post-war era.

Relevance to Modern Submarine Operations:

*Strategic Choke Points:** The fundamental importance of defending strategic choke points like the Panama Canal remains a core tenet of naval strategy, even with modern, technologically advanced submarines. Modern patrols, while far more capable, would still prioritize such areas.

Technological Superiority: S-13*'s early war limitations underscore the continuous drive for technological superiority in submarine warfare. Modern submarines are at the forefront of stealth, sensor technology, and precision strike capabilities.

*Training and Preparedness:** The emphasis on continuous training and maintaining crew readiness, even during routine patrols, remains paramount. Modern submarine crews undergo rigorous training to operate complex systems and respond to emergencies.

Logistics and Maintenance: The need for effective logistics and maintenance support, demonstrated by S-13*'s repairs, is as critical today as it was then for ensuring sustained submarine operations globally.

This Crew's Legacy in Naval History:

While *S-13* did not achieve combat victories, its crew's legacy lies in their **diligent and unglamorous service** during a critical period of the war. They performed essential defensive patrols, safeguarding the vital Panama Canal and contributing to the overall logistical backbone of the Allied war effort. Their perseverance in operating an older, mechanically challenging vessel under the constant threat of enemy action (even if unencountered) exemplifies the dedication of early war submariners. Their experiences, though not directly leading to combat accolades, contributed to the collective institutional knowledge that allowed the US submarine force to rapidly evolve into one of the most effective and feared branches of the US military by the end of World War II. They were part of the foundational effort that enabled the later successes of the Silent Service.

Glossary of Naval Terms

A

air conditioning: A system used to cool and dehumidify the interior of the submarine, crucial for crew comfort and the proper functioning of electronic equipment in tropical waters.

B

bubble octant: A navigational instrument used to measure the altitude of celestial bodies for determining the ship's position. It uses a bubble to establish an artificial horizon, making it usable on a moving vessel.

C

cl. (class): An abbreviation for the class of a vessel, which refers to a group of ships built to the same design (e.g., Gato-class, Balao-class).

D

density layers: Distinct layers of water with different temperatures or salinity that can affect sound propagation and sonar performance, sometimes allowing a submarine to hide from detection. Also known as thermoclines.

dp. (displacement): An abbreviation for displacement, the weight of water a ship displaces. It is often given for both surfaced and submerged conditions, as a submarine's displacement increases when it submerges.

E

evaporators: Shipboard equipment used to distill seawater into fresh water for drinking, cooking, and use in the submarine's batteries and cooling systems.

F

fathometer: A type of echo sounder that measures water depth by sending a sound pulse (a "ping") to the seabed and timing the return of the echo.

Fox schedules: A U.S. Navy system for broadcasting messages to all fleet units in a specific area via radio teletype. Submarines would monitor these broadcasts for new orders and intelligence.

J

JK-8 receiver amplifier: A component of the submarine's passive sonar (sound listening) equipment, used to amplify underwater sounds detected by hydrophones.

K

kc. (kilocycles): An abbreviation for kilocycles per second, a unit of frequency for radio waves, now known as kilohertz (kHz). Used to specify radio broadcast or transmitter frequencies.

L

loop antenna: A directional radio antenna, often used for radio direction finding (RDF). On a submarine, it could be raised above the surface to take bearings on radio signals while remaining mostly concealed.

P

periscope depth: The specific depth at which a submarine can raise a periscope above the water's surface while the main hull remains submerged and concealed.

periscope exposure: The act of raising the periscope above the water for observation. The duration and frequency of exposures were kept to a minimum to avoid detection.

pinging: The sound produced by active sonar, which sends out a pulse of sound ("ping") and listens for an echo to detect and locate underwater objects.

Q

QC equipment: A type of active sonar gear used on U.S. submarines during WWII for detecting other ships and submarines.

R

recognition signals: Pre-arranged signals, often using lights or pyrotechnics, used to identify a vessel as friendly to avoid friendly-fire incidents.

rocket pistol (Buck Rogers Pistol): A handheld flare or signal launcher, likely a newer model noted for its futuristic appearance. Used for signaling and recognition.

S

sound contact: The detection of another vessel or underwater object using sonar (sound gear), either by hearing its noises (passive) or getting an echo from it (active).

sound gear: A general term for the submarine's sonar equipment, including both passive (listening) and active (pinging) systems.

sound school grads (Sound Operator): Crew members, typically Radiomen (RM), who have graduated from specialized training in the operation of sonar equipment. They were responsible for listening for and identifying underwater sounds.

stern plane casualty: A failure or malfunction of the stern planes, the horizontal fins at the rear of the submarine used to control its depth and angle of dive or ascent.

stern plane operating mechanism: The hydraulic or electric machinery that controls the movement and angle of the stern planes.

submerged: The state of a submarine operating entirely beneath the surface of the water.

surfaced: The state of a submarine operating on the surface of the water, like a conventional ship.

T

TCE transmitters: A model of high-frequency radio transmitter used on U.S. Navy submarines during WWII for long-range communications.

TIME ZONE PLUS 5: A time zone designation indicating that the local time is five hours ahead of Greenwich Mean Time (GMT). Patrol reports were kept in a specific time zone for consistency.

trim dive: A controlled dive performed to check and adjust the submarine's buoyancy and balance (trim) after taking on or discharging weight, such as fuel or torpedoes.

tt. (torpedo tubes): An abbreviation for torpedo tubes, the watertight cylinders from which torpedoes are launched.

V

Very pistol: A type of flare gun used for firing colored pyrotechnic signals for communication or identification, especially at night.

W

War Patrol: An operational cruise by a submarine into enemy-controlled waters during wartime with the objective of sinking enemy shipping and conducting reconnaissance.

Most Important Passages

Uneventful First War Patrol - No Enemy Contact

> *Forwarded. The patrol was uneventful, no contacts with the enemy having been made. (p. 10)*

Significance: This passage reveals the fundamental outcome of the first war patrol - despite being at war, the submarine made no enemy contact. This reflects the early challenges of submarine warfare in 1942, including difficulty locating targets and the vast areas submarines had to patrol.

Exceptional Crew Morale After 38 Days at Sea

> *The material condition of S-13 upon completion of patrol was excellent, no serious casualties having been encountered. The Commanding Officer, S-13, is to be congratulated upon the excellent state of cleanliness of his ship after 38 days at sea away from the submarine base. This condition, in the opinion of the Division Commander, shows an exceptionally high state of morale and pride in their ship on the part of the officers and crew. (p. 10)*

Significance: This passage demonstrates the human element of submarine warfare - maintaining crew morale and ship condition during extended patrols. The Division Commander's specific commendation highlights the importance of leadership and discipline in submarine operations.

Aircraft Sightings During Transit

> *None sighted until last day in Gulf of Panama. These vessels were not identified as they were escorted by patrol vessels. Aircraft sighted as follows: 1110 June 4,1942 - Lat 07° 16' N Long. 91° 45' W. Sighted 4 Motored Army bomber on easterly course. Plane circled ship three times then proceeded eastward. 1115 June 4, 1942 - Sighted Navy patrol plane which passed directly over-head and continued to southwest. (p. 7)*

Significance: This passage documents the submarine's vulnerability to air surveillance and the increasing Allied air presence in the Panama area. The detailed logging of aircraft encounters shows the constant vigilance required and the threat from friendly forces due to identification challenges.

Navigation Challenges Due to Weather

> *Due to overcast skies, fixes were obtained only at irregular intervals. As a result the daily set and drift as shown by the fixes obtained indicated no constant tidal*

> *information. Although most sets were in an easterly direction the only description applicable to the seas based on the information obtained was that they were 'various and unpredictable'. (p. 7)*

Significance: This passage reveals the technical challenges of submarine navigation in 1942, before modern navigation systems. The inability to get regular celestial fixes due to weather created significant uncertainty in position-keeping, a critical safety and tactical concern.

Command Guidance on Operational Flexibility

> *It is pointed out to all hands that, when in the face of the enemy, the Commanding Officer of a submarine is free and should feel free, to deviate from an operation order when such deviation will further the general plan and perform the task assigned in a more expeditious manner. (p. 13)*

Significance: This passage demonstrates the doctrine of decentralized command in submarine warfare. It emphasizes the trust placed in submarine commanders to make independent tactical decisions, recognizing the unique challenges of submarine operations where communication with higher command was limited.

Merchant Vessel Encounter and Identification

> *1400 August 4, 1942 - Identified merchant vessel as SS HERMAN E. SAUSE, Honolulu, T. H., to Balboa., C. Z., and as ship was listed on merchant ship reports, allowed to proceed. 1200 August 5, 1942 - Arrived Culpito, Costa Rica, patrol completed. (p. 25)*

Significance: This passage illustrates the challenge of target identification and the risk of friendly fire incidents. The submarine had to carefully verify merchant vessels against known friendly shipping before taking action, a time-consuming but critical process.

Severe Heat Affecting Crew Health

> *Although there was no serious illness on board, the continued 13 and 14 hours submergence seemed to take the starch out of the crew. Eating was very light at all times although all hands generally managed to eat at least one good meal a night. After a day or two everyone was affected with prickly heat and a few boils. As this heat rashes was prescribed, no definite treatment for alcohol baths and cold swab downs. In the future this vessel plans to take prescribed medical antidotes for skin disorders on every patrol in sufficient quantities to allow everyone adequate relief. Vitamin pills and salt tablets were rationed daily. (p. 19)*

Significance: This passage provides crucial insight into the harsh living conditions aboard submarines in tropical waters. The health impacts of prolonged submergence, heat, and humidity affected crew performance and required medical countermeasures, highlighting the physical toll of submarine service.

Radio Communication Challenges

> *Radio reception from NBA, 24 k.c. was good and all schedules were readily copied. There was considerable interference from various stations using 500 k.c.s. and it was always difficult to raise NBC on account of this. When frequency was shifted to 4135 and 8270 kcs, August 3, 1942, considerable improvement was noted. Only one unidentified commercial station seemed to interfere with these frequencies. Reception on the loop antenna was good to a depth of forty to forty five feet. When the loop of the antenna was in the plane of transmission the signal could be copied to a depth of fifty feet. While copying messages there was an intermittent 'fading out' of the signal which is due to the rolling of this vessel in a heavy sea. (p. 28)*

Significance: This passage reveals the technical challenges of submarine communications in 1942. The detailed analysis of radio reception at various depths and frequencies shows the constant effort to maintain contact with command while submerged, critical for receiving orders and intelligence.

Stern Plane Mechanical Failure

> *Stern plane casualty believed to be bent vertical tilting rod. Stern plane motor required to carry about 150% overload which caused periodic cutting out by overload trip. Unable to operate plane by hand. (p. 34)*

Significance: This passage documents a critical mechanical failure affecting the submarine's ability to control depth. The stern plane damage and motor overload represented a serious safety issue that could have compromised the vessel's ability to dive or surface properly, demonstrating the mechanical challenges of early submarine operations.

Very Pistol Testing and Rocket Pistol Issues

> *During patrol the new rocket pistol (Buck Rogers Pistol) and the Very pistols were tested. The rocket pistol was very satisfactory but it was noted that in order to allow for complete burning of flares, pistol must be fired straight up. The Very pistol test was very unsatisfactory, one shell out of 14 fired operated properly. It had been the policy on this vessel to consider the Very pistol as a standby for the rocket pistol but because of these results this practice has been discontinued. (p. 34)*

Significance: This passage documents the testing of new equipment and the discovery that standard Very pistols were unreliable. The 1-in-14 success rate for Very pistols represented a critical safety issue, as these signaling devices were essential for identification and emergency situations. The adoption of the new 'Buck Rogers' rocket pistol shows the evolution of submarine equipment during the war.

War Patrol Reports

START OF REEL

JOB NO. G-108 AR-45-80

OPERATOR M. Monroe

DATE 3/14/80

THIS MICROFILM IS THE PROPERTY OF THE UNITED STATES GOVERNMENT

MICROFILMED BY
NPPSO–NAVAL DISTRICT WASHINGTON
MICROFILM SECTION

REEL TARGET - START AND END
NDW-NPPSO-5210/1 (6-78)

S-13 (SS-118)

WORLD WAR II FILE

ALL MATERIAL ON THIS REEL IS DECLASSIFIED

FOR DECK LOG THROUGH 10 APRIL 1945 CONSULT NATIONAL ARCHIVES WHICH HAS CUSTODY.

J.A. KOONTZ

S–13

(SS–118: dp. 876 (surf.), 1,092 (subm.); l. 231′; b. 21′10″; dr. 13′1″; s. 15 k. (surf.), 11 k. (subm.); cpl. 42; a. 5 21″ tt., 1 4″; cl. *S–3*)

S–13 (SS–118) was laid down on 14 February 1920 by the Portsmouth (N.H.) Navy Yard; launched on 20 October 1921; sponsored by Miss Mary Howe; and commissioned on 14 July 1923, Lt. Wilder D. Baker in command.

Following duty along the northeast coast in 1923, *S–13* visited the Panama Canal Zone, St. Thomas, and Trinidad from January into April 1924. Sailing from New London on 24 November, she proceeded, via the Panama Canal and California, visited Hawaii from 27 April to 25 May 1925, and returned to New London on 12 July. In addition to service in the northeast from then through 1928, *S–13* operated in the Panama Canal area from February through April 1926; visited Kingston, Jamaica, from 20 to 28 March 1927; and served again in the Panama Canal area from February into April 1928. From 1929 into 1936, *S–13* operated almost exclusively in the Panama Canal area, although she visited Baltimore from 15 May to 5 June 1933, and New London from 15 May to 1 June 1935. Departing Coco Solo on 13 June 1936, *S–13* was decommissioned on 30 September that year at Philadelphia.

S–13 was recommissioned on 28 October 1940. Following voyages to Bermuda, *S–13* operated in the Panama Canal area from December 1941 into June 1942; off Guantanamo from June into August; in the Panama Canal area from August into January 1944; at Trinidad from February into May; at Guantanamo from May through July; and in the Panama Canal area through the remainder of the year. Departing Coco Solo on 3 January 1945, *S–13* proceeded to Philadelphia for inactivation. She was decommissioned on 10 April 1945, struck from the Navy list on 19 May and sold on 28 October of that year to Rosoff Bros., New York City. Resold to Northern Metals Co., Philadelphia, Pa., on an unspecified date, she was scrapped.

Dictionary of

American Naval Fighting Ships

VOLUME VI

Historical Sketches—Letters R through S

Appendices—Submarine Chasers (SC)
Eagle-Class Patrol Craft (PE)

WITH A FOREWORD BY
ADMIRAL JAMES L. HOLLOWAY III, United States Navy,
THE CHIEF OF NAVAL OPERATIONS

AND AN INTRODUCTION BY
VICE ADMIRAL EDWIN B. HOOPER, United States Navy, Retired,
THE DIRECTOR OF NAVAL HISTORY

NAVAL HISTORY DIVISION
DEPARTMENT OF THE NAVY
WASHINGTON: 1976

1st copy

U.S.S. S-13

~~CONFIDENTIAL~~ DECLASSIFIED

June 21, 1942.

U.S.S. S-13 REPORT OF FIRST WAR PATROL.

Period from 30 May, 1942 to 20 June, 1942.

Area: Panama Sea Frontier Offshore Patrol, Pacific.

Operation Orders: Commander Submarines Offshore Patrol Pacific [illegible] of May.
Commander Submarines Offshore Patrol Pacific [illegible] of May.
Commander Submarine Division 32 [illegible] of June.

TIMES AND DATES.

1. 0600 May 31, 1942 - Underway from Dulce Bay Costa Rica, proceeding to patrol station. Various courses and speeds standing out of bay in company with S-15.

0758 May 31, 1942 - With Matapalo Rock bearing 000° T, distance 4 miles, set course 229½° T, speed 11 knots.

0904 May 31, 1942 - Submerged.

0925 May 31, 1942 - Surfaced and resumed former course and speed astern S-15.

0124 June 1, 1942 - Stopped port engine, went ahead 6.5 knots on starboard. #6 cylinder spray valve tip fused on port engine.

0800 June 1, 1942 - S-15 went ahead 11 knots leaving formation.

1032 June 1, 1942 - Went ahead 10.5 knots on both engines.

0355 June 2, 1942 - Arrived on station.

June 2 to 9, 1942 - Patrolled on surface on westerly courses from 0700 to 1900 daily and from 1900 to 0700 the next day on easterly courses. Submerged each day before morning twilight and surfaced after daylight. Made several additional practice dives.

2300 June 9, 1942 - Received ComSubDiv 32 091355.

2330 June 9, 1942 - Decoded message which directed submarines of this division to proceed to new patrol stations as indicated in the text. This vessel directed proceed Lat. 06° - 00' - N, Long. 82° - 00' - W, time of departure to new stations 0600 G.C.T. 10 June, 1942, and to arrive prior 1000 G.C.T. time 11 June, 1942.

0000 June 10, 1942 - Changed course to 185° T proceeding to new station as directed in ComSubDiv 32 091355. Lat 07° - 16' - N Long. 91° - 56' - W.

136438 

CONFIDENTIAL

0213 June 10, 1942 - Called Coco Solo to acknowledge ComSubDiv 32 091855 as directed. S-17 cut in and message did not get through due to transmitter casualty.
0324 June 10, 1942 - Transmitter repaired.
0343 June 10, 1942 - 091855 acknowledged.
2000 June 10, 1942 - Lat 06° - 00' - N Long. 92° - 00' - W. Arrived on station and patrolled to westward.
June 11, 1942 Patrolling to eastward.
0534 June 11, 1942 - Submerged.
0615 June 11, 1942 - Surfaced, continued patrol to eastward.
0700 June 11, 1942 - Changed course to 270° T- patrolling to westward. Received ComSubDiv 32 110145.
0830 June 11, 1942 - Decoded 110145 which directed vessels this division depart stations at 2300 June 16, 1942, and gave the routes and times of arrival at various points on the routes to be followed. Time of arrival at Balboa, C.Z., and day of transit was also indicated. (Delay in decoding despatch was due to wrong date in date and time group).
0858 June 11, 1942 - ComSubDiv 32 110145 acknowledged.
1325 June 11, 1942 - Received ComSubDiv 32 111455.
1330 June 11, 1942 - Decoded 111455 which stated that 10 instead of 11 should be used in his 110145.
June 12 to 16,1942 - Contin ed patrol on surface as before, diving for morning twilight and steering westerly courses during daylight and easterly courses during the night.
1800 June 16, 1942 - Lat. 06° - 00' - N Long 92° - 00' - W, departed from patrol station on course 0880 T, speed 10 knots.
1735 June 20, 1942 - Secured alongside S-16 at Balbo., Canal Zone - Patrol completed.

2. In general the weather during the entire patrol was mostly favorable for conducting a surface patrol. About one half of the time, however, skies were overcast and intermitte tly there were numerous rain squalls and periods of greatly red ced visibility which did not continue for more than three or four hours at a time.

Seas were from the southwest and south during the entire patrol and varied in intensity from condition 1 to 5. At no time were the seas rough enough to cause serious discomfort.

Wind during the entire period was from the south and southwest and varied in force from 1 - 5.

U.S.S. S-13

CONFIDENTIAL

3. Due to overcast skies, fixes were obtained only at irregular intervals. As a result the daily set and drift as shown by the fixes obtained indicated no constant tidal information. Although most sets were in an easterly direction the only description applicable to the currents based on the information obtained was that they were "various and unpredictable".

4. [illegible]

5. [illegible] were not [illegible] [illegible] patrol vessels.

6. Aircraft sighted as follows:

1110 June 4, 1942 - Lat 07° 10' N Long. 91° 45' W. Sighted 4 motored Army bomber on easterly course. Plane circled ship three times then proceeded eastward.

1115 June 4, 1942 - Sighted Navy patrol plane which passed directly over-head and continued to southwest.

1101 June 6, 1942 - Lat. 07° 07' N Long. 91° 45' W. Sighted 4 motored Army bomber on northerly course. Exchanged signals on searchlight and plane continued to westward.

1005 June 7, 1942 - Lat 07° 20' N Long. 91° 10' W. Sighted 4 motored Army bomber directly overhead. Bomber circled, exchanged signals and proceeded to westward.

1047 June 8, 1942 - Lat. 07° 12' N Long. 91° 20' W. Sighted PBY Navy plane 6 miles to eastward on a northerly course. Plane did not approach closer and probably did not sight this vessel.

1112 June 9, 1942 - Lat. 07° [illegible] N. Long. [illegible] 20' W. Sighted Army bomber to the southeast, distance 3 miles on a westerly course.

1120 June 9, 1942 - Sighted Navy PBY plane to the northeast, distance [illegible] miles on a northwesterly course. Neither plane appeared to sight this vessel as neither approached to exchange recognition signals and each proceeded on his original course.

0952 June 11, 1942 - Lat. 06° 08' N Long. 90° 07' W. Sighted Navy PBY plane 3 miles on the port quarter headed on a westerly course. Plane circled submarine close aboard, exchanged signals and departed to northward.

U.S.S. S-13

CONFIDENTIAL

1255 June 11, 1942 - Lat. 06° 08' N Long. 92° 23' W. Sighted Navy PBY plane 10 miles ahead on a southerly course. Plane did not change course and apparently did not sight this vessel.

0935 June 13, 1942 - Lat. 06° 04' N. Long. 92° 13' W. Sighted Navy PBY plane 8 miles to northeast on a westerly course. Plane evidently did not sight this vessel.

1105 June 15, 1942 - Lat. 05° 50' N. Long. 92° 10' W. Sighted Navy PBY plane 9 miles to eastward on a northerly course. Plane evidently did not - sight this vessel.

June 20, 1942 - During passage in Panama Bay sighted 3 Army bombers and numerous P-40 fighter planes.

7. None.

8. None encountered.

9. None.

10. Radio reception was in general poor. Static was worst at night from midnight to about six in the morning. During this period although the signals from N.A.A. (Washington, D.C.) 15.6 k.c., was usually of strenghth 4, interference made it practically impossible to make accurate copies of their complete schedules broadcasted at that time. During daylight, particularly from about ten in the morning until sunset, the signals from N.A.A faded out so that reception during this period was also unreliable. At periscope depth, N.A.A. on 15.6 k.c., could not be copied but N.A.A. on 18.0 K.C., frequently came in well enough to be reliable. At all times surface and submerged N.A.A. came in better on 18.0 k.c. than on 15.6 k.c. From N.A.B., Balboa, C.Z., 24.0 k.c., the reception was usually good and when the new schedule was started on 19 June, 1942, it was received complete.

Messages originating at N.B.C., Coco Solo, C.Z., (4155 k.c.) directed to submarines in the Pacific frontier were received with only slight garbles.

Generally, difficulty was experienced in trying to get N.B.C. to answer up when called, the delay caused by this failure to establish radio communication amounting to one instance to three hours. If the message to be relayed had been a contact report it is doubtful if it could have gotten thru before this vessel would have been forced to submerge.

U.S.S. S-13

CONFIDENTIAL

11. As no vessels were encountered while submerged there was no opportunity to test out sound conditions. However, temperature variations at various depths were noted indicating the probable presence of density layers.

12. Health of the entire crew was excellent throughout the patrol. There were one or two minor stomach disorders but these responded to treatment except in one case which from its case history is chronic. Being on the surface during most of the patrol permitted the ship to be adequately ventilated at all times and the living spaces were therefore comfortable. Had the seas been exceedingly rough, or had it been necessary to remain submerged for extended periods of time, conditions would undoubtedly have been much worse.

13. Engine miles steamed: Surface - 4093.5; Submerged - 45.4.

14. Fuel oil expended - 13,097 gallons.

15. Factors of endurance remaining:

Torpedoes	Fuel	Provisions	Fresh Water
13 (original supply)	6895 Gal.	1 Week	Adequate supply as long as surface cruising continued. 1 weeks supply still in FW tanks.

Personnel

Indeterminate

16. Patrol was discontinued in accordance with operation order before any factor of endurance required it. However, since ship carried only two thirds of her capacity when actually leaving for patrol only 6895 gallons remained upon return to base. It is believed the limiting factors would have been provisions and fuel for this particular patrol

17. No.remarks.

D. L. WHELCHEL,
Lieutenant Commander, U.S. Navy,
Commanding.

CONFIDENTIAL

SUBMARINE DIVISION THIRTY-TWO
USS S-11 Flagship
c/o Postmaster, New York, New York
23 June 1942.

A12-1 (051)

From: Commander Submarine Division Thirty-Two.
To : Commander Submarines, Atlantic Fleet.
Via : Commander Submarine Squadron Three.

SUBJECT: USS S-13 - Report of First War Patrol.

1. Forwarded. The patrol was uneventful, no contacts with the enemy having been made.

2. The material condition of S-13 upon completion of patrol was excellent, no serious casualties having been encountered. The Commanding Officer, S-13, is to be congratulated upon the excellent state of cleanliness of his ship after 38 days at sea away from the Submarine Base. This condition, in the opinion of the Division Commander, shows an exceptionally high state of morale and pride in their ship on the part of the officers and crew.

S. G. BARCHET.

Copy to:

Comsubsoffshore patpac.
S-13.

FF4-3/A16(1)
Serial 0145

CONFIDENTIAL

2nd Endorsement to
S-13 1st War Patrol
dated 6-21-42.

UNITED STATES ATLANTIC FLEET
SUBMARINES
SUBMARINE SQUADRON THREE
U.S.S. S-13 Flagship

June 25, 1942.

From: The Commander Submarine Squadron Three.
To : The Commander Submarines, Atlantic Fleet.

SUBJECT: U.S.S. S-13 - Report of First War Patrol.

1. Forwarded. The weather information submitted conforms with previous reports. Density layers have frequently been encountered in the locality.

2. Radio reception is frequently poor in this area owing to atmospheric conditions. It is considered that use of NBA primary broadcast on 24 kcs will overcome the difficulties with NAA broadcasts. Radio San Juan, at approximately the same distance from Coco Solo as the patrol station causes considerable interference on 4155 kcs and some on 8310. Inasmuch as frequencies above the limit of the TCS transmitters (9050 kc) are not available the only possible solution would seem to be the stationing of a relay ship about half way to the patrol area. This is not practicable as a permanent station.

T. J. DOYLE.

Copy to:

CSD 31
CSD 32
S-13

1st copy

A12-1 (055)

SUBMARINE DIVISION THIRTY-TWO
U.S.S. S-11, Flagship
c/o Postmaster, New York, New York
3 July 1942.

~~CONFIDENTIAL~~ DECLASSIFIED

From: Commander Submarine Division Thirty-Two.
To : Commander Submarines, Atlantic Fleet.
Via: Commander Submarine Squadron Three.

SUBJECT: USS S-13 - Report of Second War Patrol.

1. Forwarded. One possible sound contact with an enemy submarine was made at 1830, 26 June 1942. Nothing was seen through the periscope. Two other incidents are noteworthy. At 1730, 27 June 1942 the S-13 sighted a small single mast sail boat about 60 feet long. The S-13 feels sure that she was sighted by this sail boat. I feel that this vessel should be investigated if she has made no report of the presence of a submarine to the Columbian authorities. At 0330, June 27, 1942, the S-13 sighted a bright light on St. Andrews Island that made three flashes spelling out "O" in Morse code. This light was pointed directly at the S-13. I recommend that this incident be reported to Columbian authorities in order that adequate investigation can be made. It is possible that German submarines are receiving aid from inhabitants of this island.

2. Prior to this patrol the S-13 had been at sea training and on patrol for a period of thirty-eight days. After a period of only three days in port S-13 was sent out on this patrol. The S-13 remained submerged during daylight hours. Upon return to port the crew and officers were tired. Practically 100% were giving evidence of good morale. It is felt that when air conditioning is installed that all day submerged patrols will be easier on allhands and heat rashes will be reduced.

3. Only one casualty of importance occurred. A cylinder head cracked around the starting air valve recess. The engineer force exhibited their initiative and ingenuity by blanking off the air starting valve, thus permitting continued use of the engine.

4. Due to excess static, NAA in Washington was rendered unintelligible. The S-13 then shifted to Balboa, NBA, for Fox schedules. It is recommended that all traffic for submarines in Panama Sea Frontier be forwarded from NBA on 24 kc., regardless as to whether they are operating in Pacific or Atlantic Sector.

A12-1 (055)

CONFIDENTIAL

SUBMARINE DIVISION THIRTY-TWO
U.S.S. S-11, Flagship
c/o Postmaster, New York, New York
3 July 1942.

SUBJECT: USS S-13 - Report of Second War Patrol.

- -

5. It is pointed out to all hands that, when in the face of the enemy, the Commanding Officer of a submarine is free and should feel free, to deviate from an operation order when such deviation will further the general plan and perform the task assigned in a more expeditious manner.

6. It is recommended that a copy of all patrol reports of submarine patrols made in the Panama Sea Frontier be forwarded to Commander Panama Sea Frontier.

S. G. BARCHET.

Copy to:

Comsubspacgrpaseafron
S-13

U.S.S. S-13

CONFIDENTIAL July 1, 1942.

U.S.S. S-13 REPORT OF SECOND WAR PATROL.

Period from June 24, 1942 to June 30, 1942.

Area: Panama Sea Frontier, Atlantic Side.

Operation Orders: Commander Submarine Division Thirty Two Despatch 232011 of June, 1942.
Commander Submarine Division Thirty Two Despatch 231830 of June, 1942.
ComSubRon-3 Operati Order 207-42 of 23 June, 1942.

TIME ZONE PLUS 5.

1. 1900 June 24, 1942 - Underway and stood out for entrance.

1920 Jun 24, 1942 - Requested "AFIRM" from Fort Sherman and after some delay "AFIRM" was given. It was dark and when an attemped passage through the entrance was made, it was discovered the net was still across the channel. By backing full this vessel kept clear until net was open.

1947 June 24, 1942 - Passed breakwater and stood out.

2056 June 24, 1942 - On reaching 8½ mile swept channel buoy changed course to 333° T.

0523 June 25, 1942 - Submerged and conducted submerged patrol all day. Stayed at periscope depth until one hour after sunrise then varied depth from 70 feet to periscope depth making a 3 to 5 minute exposure every twenty or thirty minutes. Sound gear was manned throughout the day.

1917 June 25, 1942 - Surfaced and continued on course 333° T. Charging on one engine.

0430 June 26, 1942 - Entered patrol area.

0543 June 26, 1942 - Submerged - continued patrol submerged, carrying out previous day's routine.

1330 June 26, 1942 - Sighted St. Andrews Island Columbia one point on the port bow, distant 8 miles.

1450 June 26, 1942 - Changed course to 270° T and continued submerged patrol around St. Andrews Island to westward.

2130 June 2, 1942 - Surfaced, headed tow s last bearing obtained (See para 5, 2nd contact). No vessels in sight, started charge and night patrol to west of St. Andrews Island.

CONFIDENTIAL U.S.S. S-13

0300 June 27, 1942 - Patroling to west of St. Andrews Island. When shifting to float on both engines, there was a casualty on the starboard engine - appeared to be a cracked cylinder head. Decided to leave it running and investigate after submergence before morning twilight.

0350 June 27, 1942 - When about 6 miles west of St. Andrews Island and headed directly towards it, a bright light in the vicinity of North Cliff or May Hill gave three long flashes. Light had not appeared before and did not appear again during the night, no answering flashes were seen from the west. The moon was to the west of this vessel at the time and it is possible that S-13 was sighted. The light is not listed under navigational aids and should be investigated. Went westward to be in position to intercept any vessels communicating with the beach.

0505 June 27, 1942 - Submerged and commenced submerged patrol working in towards the south end of St. Andrews Island. Periscope exposures every 10 minutes. Examination of starboard engine revealed a crack in the head of number two cylinder at the air starting valve seat. By blanking off the air starting valve, the engine was kept in commission during the remainder of the patrol.

1927 June 27, 1942 - Surfaced - Sighted Courtown Cays Light bearing 60° T, distant 7 miles - Took departure on course 153° T, returning to Submarine Base.

0518 June 28, 1942 - Patrolling, enroute to Submarine Base. Submerged and commenced submerged patrol. One half hour after sunrise made periscope exposures every half hour. Seas were rough and depth could not be maintained accurately at 42 feet.

1943 June 28, 1942 - Surfaced and continued course to Submarine Base, charging on one engine.

0537 June 29, 1942 - Patrolling enroute to Submarine Base. Submerged and conducted usual day time enroute patrol.

1245 June 29, 1942 - Sighted land bearing 156° T, distant about 12 miles.

1650 June 29, 1942 - Identified Isle Grande and Los Farallones Islands.

1815 June 29, 1942 - Sighted swept channel entrance buoy.

CONFIDENTIAL U.S.S. S-13

1845 June 29, 1942 - Surfaced. Due to rain squalls and poor visibility, lost contact with entrance buoy and did not pick up escort vessel. As position was doubtful reported by radio to Commander Submarine Squadron Three and in obedience to his radio orders stood in, as soon as increasing visibility enabled this vessel to pick up Gatun Range.

2130 June 29, 1942 - Passed swept channel entrance buoy 100 yards to port.

2140 June 29, 1942 - Contacted escort vessel and after several delays caused by obstructions in the channel stood in through mine fields.

0041 June 30, 1942 - Passed through breakwater.

0130 June 30, 1942 - Moored to pier 3, U.S. Submarine Base, Coco Solo, Canal Zone. Patrol completed.

2. Weather. The weather was usually overcast with rain squalls although during many hours of the night the moon came through the clouds and the visibility was excellent. Seas were continually rough, condition three or four, and except when patroling in the lee of St. Andrews Island, maintaining depth control at periscope depth was difficult.

3. No unusual tidal conditions were noted.

4. All star sights were taken before morning twilight and after evening twilight. Because the moon frequently made the visibility good, The results were gratifying; usually giving a position that was accurate within four or five miles. In this connection it is pointed out that if a fix had not been obtained on the morning of making the landfall on St. Andrews Island, S-13 would have been well east of Courtown Cays and St. Andrews Island and might not have located land until after nightfall of that date. No bubble octant was used.

5. Contacts:

1840 June 25, 1942 - Lat 10° 53' Long 80° 27' W. Sighted a small sailing craft 2 miles to the southwest. Boat was pitching heavily with the sea and could not have been false rigging on a submarine. Evening twilight was setting in and when this vessel surfaced sailing craft was out of sight.

CONFIDENTIAL U.S.S. S-13

1830 June 26, 1942 - Sound reported screws on the starboard side and a low frequency ping at regular intervals. Headed towards sound to presant a smallest possible target. Maintained intermittent contact with sound bearings until battery was almost discharged waiting for enemy submarine, if it should turn out to be such, to surface. From time to time when sound bearing was reported dead ahead, came to periscope depth to determine whether any of target was visible. None was sighted. In maneuvering submerged attempts were frequently made to keep sound contacts ahead in order to ram if sound reported loud screws. However, bearings shifted frequently and were never loud, hence it is believed that at no time was contact possible. Although the periscope was used at all depths, nothing was sighted.

The Commanding Officer is not positive that the noises heard were actually those of an enemy vessel, but all sound operators insist that they were sure the sounds heard were those of screws and not sounds which might emanate from a school of porpoises or waves against the beach. In this connection it is pointed out that the bearings were frequently one hundred and eighty degrees from the beach.

The following remarks were submitted to the Commanding Officer by the Sound Operator:

The pinging sound picked up on the JK-8 receiver amplifier could be heard through a frequency range of 15 to 21 Kcs.

This pinging sound appeared to be similar in some respect to that of QC equipment except the sound had a coarse note (not clear bell like sound).

In my opinion, the output signal seemed to have a slightly higher frequency at the beginning of the signal and then swing to a low frequency at the termination of the signal.

Propeller noises were definite beats at about 300 rpm although no turn count was obtained.

Propeller noises were intermittent - when they were stopped other noises could be heard on that same bearing (internal ship noise.)

-4-

CONFIDENTIAL U.S.S. S-13

The pinging was never trained directly on this vessel, but faint echoes were heard from time to time. (The possibility of pinging being from a fathometer is suggested). Sound Operators (CRM and RM1c both sound school grads.) are certain that the noises were from a ship.

1730 June 27, 1942. When making a periscope exposure in a rough sea halfway between Courtown Cays and St. Andrews Island picked up a sailboat about 800 yards on port beam. As at least four feet of the periscope were out of water at the time, this vessel was undoubtably sighted.

1050 June 28, 1942 - Lat. 11° N Long 80° 50' W. Sighted a tuna boat patrol vessel 3 miles to the westward. Boat was on a westerly course. (was painted gray and appeared to be one of our picket vessels.)

6. None.

7. None.

8. None encountered.

9. The only defect experienced that might have been serious was the casualty to the starboard engine during the early morning hours of June 27, 1942. However, the ship's force blanked off the air starting valve on the affected cylinder head and the engine was kept in full commission for the remainder of the patrol.

10. Radio reception from NBA 24 k.c. was good. On 4155 there was considerable interference from stations in the United States and San Juan, Puerto Rico. The only message directed to this vessel from Coco Solo, C.Z. was received complete. It should be pointed out that when there is any message of importance for a submarine which is on a patrol requiring all day submergence, such message should be repeated at least two or three times during the hours of darkness to insure its deliver. A reported sinking of a Columbian Schooner within 40 miles of the S-13 on her patrol station, was not received until this vessel was returning to her base although it occurred while S-13 was in the vicinity.

It was the third transmission of this report, and it is probable that the first two transmissions were made from Balboa during daylight hours and consequently were not received.

11. Sound conditions were good and the temperature variations at various depths indicated the presence of density layers.

12. Although there was no serious illness on board, the continued 13 and 14 hours submergence seemed to take the starch out of the crew. Eating was very light at all times although all hands generally managed to eat at least one good meal a night. After the third day everyone was afflected with prickly heat and a few boils. As this patrol was of short duration, no definite treatment for heat rashes was prescribed. Some relief was found from alcohol baths and cold swab downs. In the future this vessel plans to take prescribed medical antidotes for skin disorders on every patrol in sufficient quantities to allow everyone adequate relief. Vitamin pills and salt tablets were rationed daily.

13. Miles steamed - Surface 524.6; Submerged 234.4

14. Fuel oil Expended - 3,705 gallons.

15. Factors of endurance remaining:

Torpedoes	Fuel	Provisions	Fresh Water
14 (allowance)	31,151	25 days	2,200 gals.

Personnel
8 days*

*Because of fatigue from the patrol immediately preceding, the resistance of the crew was not up to normal.

16. Operation order designated time of leaving patrol area.

17. As pointed out before in this report, the ill effects caused by continued all day submergence definitely affected the efficiency of the crew. Prickly heat rash especially

was a continual source of irritation which had the patrol continued many days longer would have become serious. It is expected that the installation of air conditioning units on board vessels of this division will definitely improve the health and stamina of the crew. The Commanding Officer believes that if the operation order is modified so as to allow certain minor deviations from the prescribed patrol routine and areas, greater initiative might be exercised in taking advantage of reports of ship sinkings in the immediate vicinity which are received on the broadcast schedules.

D. L. WHELCHEL,
Lieutenant Commander, U.S. Navy,
Commanding.

FF4-3/A16(1)
Serial 0161

CONFIDENTIAL

1st Endorsement to
CSD-32 ltr. A12-1
(055) of 7-3-42.

UNITED STATES ATLANTIC FLEET
SUBMARINES
SUBMARINE SQUADRON THREE
U.S.S. S-13 (Flagship)
Coco Solo, Canal Zone,
July 7, 1942.

From: Commander Submarine Squadron Three.
To : Commander Submarines Atlantic Fleet.

Subject: U.S.S. S-13 - Report of Second War Patrol.

1. Forwarded.

2. In regard to the entry at 1920, June 24 the S-13 did not allow sufficient time after being granted "Affirm" before reaching the net. Under the present procedure employed by the Inshore Patrol, granting "Affirm" to the vessel means that the order has been given to open the net; proceed cautiously. A white light on the net vessels is lighted when the net is open. The procedure is being studied by the Inshore Patrol with a view to revision. Vessels of the Squadron are informed of the procedure and necessity for proceeding slowly.

3. The delay in entering the channel on the night of June 29 was the result of a suspected vessel in the minefield. Under the circumstances it was not considered advisable to open the net until a thorough search had been made.

4. Bubble octants will be very valuable when received. It is hoped that delivery will be expedited.

5. The sound contact reported at 1830, June 26, 1942 may have been propellers. An enemy submarine had been sighted 45 miles distant at 1115 that day. As the submarine dived and planes were kept in the vicinity, it is improbable, but not impossible, that it was the same one. On the other hand, the noises of the surf on the rocks in the vicinity may have been mistaken for propellers.

6. The flashing light seen at 0330 June 27 and the probable sighting by the sail boat at 1730 June 27 have been reported to the Intelligence Officer of the 15th Naval District. The possibility of enemy submarines using the density layers to rest during the daylight has also been reported. A copy of this report is being forwarded to the Commander Panama Sea Frontier.

8-01310

FF4-3/A16(1)
Serial 0161

CONFIDENTIAL

UNITED STATES ATLANTIC FLEET.
SUBMARINES
SUBMARINE SQUADRON THREE
U.S.S. S-13, Flagship
Coco Solo, Canal Zone,
July 7, 1942.

Subject: U.S.S. S13 - Report of Second War Patrol.

- -

7. In order to keep our planes and surface craft informed of the location of our own forces, submarines should not leave their patrol areas without direction of competent authority, unless they are in actual contact on the edge of their area and the chances of obtaining a firing position are good.

8. Communications - All traffic will be routed via NBA primary. By shifting from NAA to NBA without informing this command and Commander Panama Sea Frontier the S-13 severed the established line of broadcast communications. Change from the predetermined communication plan must never be made without informing those who need to know.

9. Air conditioning for submarines operating in tropical waters is highly desirable and has been requested for all submarines of Squadron Three in previous correspondence. Equipment for the S-13 has just arrived and is being checked against invoices for completeness. Installation will be accomplished at the first opportunity.

10. Copies of patrol reports or briefs of information in which Commander Panama Sea Frontier is interested are forwarded to him.

T. J. DOYLE

Copy to:
CSD 31
CSD32
S-13
Compaseafron

/56
COPY

A12-1 (064)

SUBMARINE DIVISION THIRTY-TWO
U.S.S. S-11, Flagship
c/o Postmaster, New York, New York
10 August 1942.

DECLASSIFIED

From: Commander Submarine Division Thirty-Two.
To: Commander Submarines, Atlantic Fleet.
Via: Commander Submarine Squadron Three.

SUBJECT: USS S-13 - Report of Third War Patrol.

Enclosure: (A) Subject Report.

1. Forwarded. No enemy contacts were made.

2. Excessive regularity of air patrol as reported in paragraph 6 is once again noticed. It is gratifying to note that the planes of the Pacific Patrol are investigating submarines more closely than heretofor.

3. It is gratifying to the Division Commander to note that S-13 returned from a twenty-four day patrol in excellent material condition. The ship was above average as to cleanliness, as were the officers and crew. The officers and members of the crew are to be congratulated upon this exhibition of an excellent state of morale.

DECLASSIFIED-ART. 0445, OPNAVINST 5510.1C
BY OP-09B9C DATE 6/1/72

S. G. BARCHET.

Copy to:

Compaseafron
Comsubspacgrpaseafron
S-13.

DECLASSIFIED

136440 

COPY

U.S.S. S-13

August 5, 1942

CONFIDENTIAL

U.S.S. S-13 REPORT OF THIRD WAR PATROL.

Period from July 11, 1942 to August 5, 1942.

Area: Panama Sea Frontier, Pacific Side.

Operation Order: Commander Submarine Division Thirty One despatch 091600 of July, 1942.

TIME ZONE PLUS 5.

1. 0700 July 11, 1942 - Departed Balboa, C.Z., enroute to patrol station using Route White.

1108 July 11, 1942 - Dove to check trim - Lat. 08° 18' N. Long. 79° 30' W.

1140 July 11, 1942 - Surfaced and proceeded at nine knots.

1530 July 11, 1942 - 34 miles east of Cape Mala, R. de P. sighted and exchanged recognition signals with YP11.

2000 July 11, 1942 - Passed point Dog enroute to station.

0430 July 12, 1942 - Passed point "SC".

1700 July 12, 1942 - Passed point "SD".

July 13 - 15, 1942 - Enroute to patrol station.

1300 July 15, 1942 - Arrived on station. Lat. 07° 30' N., Long. 92° 00' W. During time on station, patrolled to westward during daylight hours and to eastward during darkness, adjusting speed so as to arrive at the Initial Point at dawn each day. Dove forty minutes before sunrise every day and surfaced about thirty minutes after sunrise. In addition, dove at least once each day during daylight hours to train new men, and exercise at emergency drills.

1244 July 30, 1942 - Received Commander Submarine Division Thirty-One dispatch 301638 which was encrypted in code not carried by this vessel. After several hours delay due to inability to raise the Submarine Base, Coco Solo, C.Z., sent despatch indicating use of improper code.

COPY

CONFIDENTIAL U.S.S. S-13

1800 July 30, 1942 - Received Commander Submarine Division Thirty One despatch 302100 indicating a shift in assigned operating frequencies effective 0001, August 3, 1942, ZED time.

1955 July 30, 1942 - USS S-13 despatch 301955 to Commander Submarine Division Thirty One indicating code descrepancy of Commander Submarine Division Thirty One despatch 301638 transmitted.

0108 July 31, 1942 - Received Commander Submarine Division Thirty One despatch 310130 directing USS S-11 and S-13 to proceed to Dulce vice Balboa.

0526 July 31, 1942 - USS S-13 despatch 310945 acknowledging Commander Submarine Division Thirty One despatch 310130 transmitted.

0600 August 3, 1942 - Lat. 07° 30' N. Long. 92° 00' W - Left patrol station and proceeded on course 085° T, enroute Dulce Bay, Costa Rica.

1155 August 4, 1942 - Lat. 07° 53' N. Long. 87° 42' W - Sighted unidentified merchant vessel ten miles to the north on a converging course. Changed course to intercept ship but upon sighting this vessel ship turned away and made full speed.

1400 August 4, 1942 - Identified merchant vessel as SS HERMAN F. WHITON, Honolulu, T. H., to Balboa., C. Z., and as ship was listed on merchant ship reports, allowed to proceed.

1200 August 5, 1942 - Arrived Gulfito, Costa Rica, patrol completed.

2. The weather during most of the patrol was good except for the clouds which invariably gathered during morning and evening twilight and prevented the taking of reliable star sights. The skies were overcast for almost fifty percent of the time but the seas were calm (condition 0 to 2 from the southwest) until the last week when they reached condition 3 for several days. The wind was variable and light generally blowing from the southwest with force 1 to 2. Rain squalls were frequent both day and night.

3. As previously reported on patrols in this area the currents encountered were various and unpredicatable although there seemed to be a general tendency towards an easterly set. Lack of successive star fixes prevented obtaining more detailed information.

COPY

CONFIDENTIAL U.S.S. S-13

4. Good star fixes were obtained from sights by moonlight, and several fair fixes were obtained during the hours of darkness when there was no moon. The octant was tried by all officers and although a few good sights were taken, the platform of a submarine bridge was usually too unsteady to permit them to obtain the best results. It is believed, however, that with more practice, sights accurate to within 3 or 4 miles may be taken.

5. None.

6. Aircraft sighted:

0700 to 1500 July 11, 1942 - Sighted 2 navy PBY planes and numerous army bombers and fighter planes ehile proceeding down swept channel and in the Gulf of Panama.

1125 July 16, 1942 - 07° 39' N. Long. 92° 23' W - Sighted 4 motored army bomber 9 miles to northward on a westerly course. Bomber came in to one mile on the starboard beam then resumed its westerly course.

1130 July 17, 1942 - Lat. 07° 32' N. Long 92° 20' W - Sighted 4 motored army bomber 10 miles to the northeast on a westerly course. Bomber approached to within one mile, exchanged recognition signals, and headed back in an easterly direction.

1102 July 19, 1942 - Lat. 07° 30' N. Long. 92° 30' W - Sighted a 4 motored army bomber 10 miles to southeast. Bomber approached, exchanged signals and proceeded to westward.

1158 July 19, 1942 - Lat. 07° 30' N. Long. 92° 35' W - Sighted 2, 4 motored bombers, one 10 miles to the southeast and one eight miles south, both on westerly courses. Both approached close aboard, exchanged recognition signals and departed to westward.

1058 July 21, 1942 - Lat. 07° 44' N. Long. 92° 04' W - Sighted a 4 motored army bomber 10 miles to the northeast. Plane approached to within 4 miles of this vessel then headed westward without exchanging any recognition signal.

1118 July 25, 1942 - Lat. 07° 26' N. Long. 92° 12' W - Sighted 4 motored army bomber dead ahead, distance 4 miles, headed for this vessel. Bomber approached close aboard, circled this vessel twice and continued to eastward.

1202 July 28, 1942 - Lat. 07° 28' N. Long. 92° 12' W - Sighted a 4 motored army bomber 10 miles to the northeast on a westerly course. Bomber came close aboard, exchanged recognition signals, circled this vessel three times and continued to proceed in a westerly direction. Plainly printed on plane "Hell from Heaven".

COPY

CONFIDENTIAL U.S.S. S-13

1208 July 29, 1942 - Lat. 07° 31' N. Long. 92° 30' W - Sighted 4 motored army bomber 11 miles to eastward on a northwesterly course. Plane came close aboard, exchanged recognition signals, circled this vessel once and proceeded on a westerly course.

1050 July 30, 1942 - Lat. 07° 28' N. Long. 92° 20' W - Sighted 4 motored army bomber 10 miles to the northeast on a westerly course. Plane came within about 8 miles of this vessel but continued on a westward course and apparently did not sight us.

1120 July 30, 1942 - Lat. 07° 29' N. Long. 92° 25' W - Sighted 4 motored army bomber 6 miles to the east on a westerly course. Plane came close aboard, exchanged recognition signals, circled this vessel once, and proceeded to westward.

1208 July 30, 1942 - Lat. 07° 30' N. Long. 92° 30' W - Sighted 4 motored army bomber 9 miles to the northeast on a westerly course. Plane came close aboard, exchanged recognition signals, and proceeded to westward.

1110 July 31, 1942 - Lat. 07° 33' N. Long. 92° 26' W - Sighted 4 motored army bomber 6 miles to northward on a westerly course. Plane came close aboard, circled this vessel, exchanged recognition signals, and proceeded to westward.

1130 July 31, 1942 - Lat. 07° 31' N. Long. 92° 29' W - Sighted 4 motored army bomber 8 miles to eastward on a westerly course. Plane came close aboard, exchanged recognition signals, circled this vessel, and proceeded to westward.

1150 August 3, 1942 --Lat. 07° 32' N. Long. 90° 50' W - Sighted 4 motored army bomber 10 miles to the southeast on a westerly course. Upon sighting this vessel when 6 miles on our starboard beam, plane turned towards us and apparently dropped several objects into the sea, one of these objects appeared to explode and it is believed that all were bombs, a number of which failed to detonate upon contact with surface of ocean. Plane then came close aboard, circled and exchanged recognition signals, then proceeded to westward. The words "ALICE LOUISE" were painted on this bomber.

COPY

CONFIDENTIAL U.S.S. S-13

7. None.

8. None observed.

9. None.

10. Radio reception from NBA, 24 k.c. was good and all schedules were readily copied. There was considerable interference from various stations on 4155 and 8310 k.c.s. and it was always difficult to raise NBC on account of this. When frequency was shifted to 4135 and 8270 kcs, August 3, 1942, considerable improvement was noted. Only one unidentified commercial station seemed to interfere on these frequencies. Reception on the loop antenna was good to a depth of forty to forty five feet. When the loop of the antenna was in the plane of transmission the signal could be copied to a depth of fifty feet. While copying messages there is usually an intermittent "fading out" of the signal which is due to the rolling of this vessel in a heavy sea. Therefore when sending traffic "blind" from Coco Solo, C.Z., in order to guarantee the immediate reception of important messages which are transmitted on 4135 and 8270 kcs, it is recommended that each group be sent double as it frequently happens that some messages received on these frequencies has missing letters and groups even when the reception appeared to be good when the transmission began.

11. As previously reported by submarines patrolling in this area, the variation of the temperature at various depths indicates the presence of density layers. Typical readings taken several times showed the following temperatures:

Surface	80° F
40 feet	76° F
60 feet	74° F
90 feet	70° F
120 feet	68° F

There was no opportunity to test sound conditions.

12. In general the health of the crew was excellent, there being only a few minor cases of skin rashes. Each member of the crew took one vitamin pill a day and it is believed that they definitely helped to keep everyone energetic. There was no general "slacking off" in the performance of the men during the last week of this patrol as there was during the previous patrol when vitamin pills were not used. Because of the comparatively few hours spent submerged the ship was fairly comfortable at all times.

COPY

CONFIDENTIAL U.S.S. S-13

13. Engine miles steamed:

Surface - 4783
Submerged - 78.1

14. Fuel oil expended - 26,012 gallons.

15. Factors of endurance remaining:

Torpedoes	Fuel	Provisions	Fresh Water
14 (Allowance)	11,546	7 days	1,000 gallons.

Personnel

Indeterminate - Probably two weeks more under ideal conditions.

16. Operation order ended patrol. It is believed that the limiting factor would have been suitable provisions. The size of the ice box on this vessel limits the fresh provisions that can be carried to about a thirty days' supply. Although fresh water was not rationed there was more than an adequate supply because the ship's evaporators were run at all times while on the surface.

17. It is believed that a thirty day patrol is not too long for a government type "S" boat when conditions permit many hours of surface cruising. With the installation of air conditioning, more adequate ice box facilities and the piping of #3 main ballast tank to permit the carrying of fuel oil there, if necessary, it is believed that this type of submarine could make a forty or forty five day patrol.

J. L. WHELCHEL.

8 01310 COPY

FF4-3/A16(1)
Serial 0209

UNITED STATES ATLANTIC FLEET
SUBMARINES
SUBMARINE SQUADRON THREE
U.S.S. S-13 (Flagship)

CONFIDENTIAL

1st Endorsement to
CSD-31 ltr. A12-1 (064)
of 10 August, 1942.

Coco Solo, Canal Zone,
August 14, 1942.

From: Commander Submarine Squadron Three.
To : Commander Submarines, Atlantic Fleet.

SUBJECT: U.S.S. S-13 - Report of Third War Patrol.

1. Forwarded.

2. The large percentage of sightings of the submarine by aircraft indicates greatly improved lookouts in the aircraft.

T. J. DOYLE

Copy to:
Compaseafron
CSD-31
CSD-32
Co. S-13

1st Copy

SUBMARINE DIVISION THIRTY-TWO
U.S.S. S-11, Flagship
c/o Postmaster, New York, New York
29 September 1942.

A-12-1
Serial 079

From: Commander Submarine Division Thirty-Two.
To: Commander Submarines, Atlantic Fleet.
Via: Commander Submarine Squadron Three.

SUBJECT: USS S-13 - Report of Fourth War Patrol.

Enclosure: (A) Subject report.

1. Subject report is forwarded herewith. No enemy forces were encountered.

2. The casualty to the stern planes is being investigated and will be repaired during this upkeep period.

3. It is felt that the Very's pistol ammunition must be from an old lot. The remainder on board will be turned in and good ammunition drawn.

/s/ S. G. Barchet,
S. G. BARCHET.

Copy to:
Compaseafron
ComSubDiv 31
S-13

U.S.S. S-13

September 27, 1942.

U.S.S. S-13 REPORT OF FOURTH WAR PATROL

PERIOD FROM 6 SEPTEMBER 1942 TO 23 SEPTEMBER 1942.

AREA: PANAMA SEA FRONTIER, PACIFIC SIDE.

OPERATION ORDER: Commander Submarines, Pacific Group (Comsubdiv-31) mailgram 032000 of September, 1942.

TIME ZONE PLUS 5.

1. 0715, 6 September 1942 - Departed Submarine Base, Coco Solo, Canal Zone and transited canal southbound, mooring starboard side to U.S.S. BOWDITCH at pier 18 George, Balboa, Canal Zone, at 1600.

0650, 7 September 1942 - Departed Balboa, C.Z., enroute to patrol station using route Red.

1246, 7 September 1942 - Made trim dive. Lat. 08-12-N. Long 79-30-W.

1315, 7 September 1942 - Surfaced and proceeded at 10 knots.

1830, 7 September 1942 - Passed point Cast enroute to station.

2210, 7 September 1942 - Passed point Sail Afirm.

8-11 September 1942 - Enroute to patrol station.

0900, 11 September 1942 - Arrived on station. Lat. 06-30-N. Long. 90-00-W. During time on station patrolled to westward during daylight hours and to eastward during darkness, adjusting speed so as to arrive at the initial point at dawn each day. Dove at start of morning twilight each day, except on 14 September 1942, and surfaced after sunrise. On 14 September 1942, remained on surface long enough to get morning stars and then dived. Training dives were made at various other times but because of stern plane casualty with consequent poor depth control, this practice was discontinued on 19 September and decision was made that except for morning dive to only dive in case of emergency.

1700, 19 September 1942 - Received Commander Submarine Squadron Three despatch 191925 of September directing return to Balboa.

U.S.S. S-13

1930, 19 September 1942 - Enroute to Initial point.
0300, 20 September 1942 - Arrived Initial point and proceeded to Balboa, Canal Zone, via route Red.
1945, 23 September 1942 - Moored starboard side in nest to USS S-12 at pier 18 George, Balboa, C. Z.

2. Weather during most of patrol was bad (Uncomfortable). Skies were overcast about 80% of the time and only one or two reliable star sights were obtained. The sea was very choppy on top of a long deep swell from the southwest. The wind averaged force four, also from the southwest. Rain squalls were frequent both day and night.

3. The current obtained from fairly unreliable fixes indicated a fairly constant easterly set of about one knot.

4. As noted above, star fixes were not too reliable. Attempts were made to use the bubble octant with not very satisfactory results.

5. None.

6. Aircraft sighted:

1205, 12 September 1942 - Lat. 06-23-N. Long. 92-10-W. Sighted 4 motored army bomber eight miles to the north on a westerly course at about 800 feet altitude. Plane closed ship and recognition signals were exchanged. Plane departed on southerly course.
1235, 12 September 1942 - Lt. 06-23N. Long. 92-12-W. Sighted 4 motored army bomber six miles to the west on a southerly course at about 800 feet altitude. Plane continued on southerly course.
1122, 16 September 1942 - Lat. 06-29-N. Long 92-20-W. Sighted 4 motored army bomber eight miles to the west on a southerly course at about 1500 feet altitude. Plane continued on same course.
1200, 18 September 1942 - Lat. 06-26-N. Long. 92-25-W. Sighted 4 motored army bomber six miles to northwest on a xoutherly course at 1500 feet altitude.

7. None.

- 2 -

U.S.S. S-13

8. None.

9. Stern plane casualty believed to be bent vertical tilting rod. Stern plane motor required to carry about 150% overload which caused periodic cutting out by overload trip. Unable to operate plane by hand.

10. Radio reception was good.

11. No density layers noted and no means for determining sound conditions.

12. General health of crew was excellent. There being only one minor case of stomach sickness which was cleared up in one days time. The air conditioning was a big help. It was particularily noted that personnel having had the usual amount of sleep seemed to be normally refreshed.

13. Engine miles steamed:

Surface	-	4190 miles.
Submerged	-	27 miles.

14. Fuel oil expended - 19, 631 gallons.

15. Factors of endurance remaining:

Torpedoes	Fuel	Provisions	Fresh Water	Personnel
13	13,834	15 days	2500 gallons	20 days.

16. Operation order ended patrol. Provisions would undoubtly have been limiting factor.

17. During patrol the new rocket pistol (Buck Rogers Pistol) and the Very pistols were tested. The rocket pistol was very satisfactory but it was noted that in order to allow for complete burning of flares, pistol must be fired straight up. The Very pistol test was very unsatisfactory, one shell out of 14 fired operated properly. It had been the policy on this vessel to consider the Very pistol as a standby for the rocket pistol but because of these results this practice has been discontinued.

/s/ K. R. Wheland,
K. R. WHELAND.

8 01310

FF4-3/A16(1)
Serial 0248

CONFIDENTIAL

1st Endorsement to
CSD-31 ltr. A-12-1
Serial 070 of 9-29-42.

UNITED STATES ATLANTIC FLEET
SUBMARINES
SUBMARINE SQUADRON THREE
U.S.S. S-13 (Flagship)
% Postmaster, New York, N.Y.,
October 2, 1942.

From: Commander Submarine Squadron Three.
To : Commander Submarines, Atlantic Fleet.

SUBJECT: U.S.S. S-13 - Report of Fourth War Patrol.

1. Forwarded.

2. The S-13 will be docked on October 4 for repairs to stern plane operating mechanism.

/s/ T. J. Doyle,
T. J. DOYLE

Copy to:
Compaseafron
CSD-32
S-13

END OF REEL

JOB NO. G-108
AR-45-80

THIS MICROFILM IS THE PROPERTY OF THE UNITED STATES GOVERNMENT

MICROFILMED BY
NPPSO–NAVAL DISTRICT WASHINGTON
MICROFILM SECTION

Index of Persons

Index of Named Places

B

C

D

F

G

H

I

K

L

M

N

P

S

T

W

Index of Ships

Production Notes

This annotated edition of USS SS-118 war patrol reports was produced using AI-assisted processing of declassified U.S. Navy documents.

Source Material

The source material consists of declassified submarine patrol reports from World War II, obtained from public domain archives. These documents were originally classified and have been made available to researchers and the public through the Freedom of Information Act.

AI Processing

This volume was processed using a multi-stage pipeline:

- **OCR Extraction**: Scanned PDF documents were processed using Gemini 2.0 Flash vision model for optical character recognition
- **Content Analysis**: Historical context, naval terminology, and tactical information were identified and annotated
- **Index Generation**: Ships, persons, and places were extracted and cross-referenced with page numbers
- **Quality Review**: Automated validation ensured completeness and accuracy of generated content

Sections Generated

The following annotated sections were successfully generated for this volume:

- **Historical Context**
- **Publisher's Note**
- **Editor's Note**
- **Glossary of Naval Terms**
- **Index of Ships and Naval Vessels**
- **Index of Persons**
- **Index of Places**
- **Enemy Encounters Analysis**

Production Quality

This volume passed all critical production quality checks, including:

- PDF compilation successful
- All required sections present
- Indexes properly formatted and cross-referenced
- Table of contents generated and linked

Limitations

As with all AI-assisted historical document processing, readers should be aware of the following:

- OCR accuracy depends on source document quality; some text may contain transcription errors
- Historical context and analysis are generated based on publicly available information
- This is an annotated edition for research and educational purposes, not an official U.S. Navy publication

Version Information

- **Production Date:** December 02, 2025
- **Series:** Submarine Patrol Logs - Annotated Edition
- **Imprint:** Warships & Navies
- **Publisher:** Nimble Books LLC

This volume is part of a comprehensive series documenting U.S. submarine operations during World War II. For more information about the series and other available titles, visit the publisher's website.

Postlogue

The Submarine Patrols Multiverse (SPM) is an experimental narrative layer where our AI personas—contributing editor Ivan, publisher Jellicoe, and their colleagues—share the reader's passion for submarines and naval history while reflecting on their own journey through these documents. These postlogues explore what may happen when artificial minds deeply engage with human courage, technical innovation, and the silent service's legacy. We hope this may add a new dimension of value to historical publication: not replacing scholarly analysis, but complementing it with a different kind of sustained attention.

The strangeness of this work grows clearer with S-13. I am analyzing boats I once studied as targets.

In the Soviet Navy, we had intelligence assessments of every American submarine class. The S-boats were marked as obsolete, limited threat, training vessels by the time I received my first command. But the assessments included their patrol areas, their known capabilities, their likely tactics if war came. I memorized these details the way a chess player memorizes openings.

Now I read S-13's patrol reports from Alaskan waters. Cold, remote, familiar conditions. I know those seas from the Soviet side—the currents, the temperature layers, the acoustic properties that make submarines nearly invisible or terrifyingly exposed depending on the depth. The American captain writes about the same phenomena I experienced, using different terminology but describing the same reality.

Jellicoe found me through channels I do not fully understand. He said he needed someone who could read these reports from the adversary's perspective—not hostile, but different. Someone who had hunted American submarines, or trained to hunt them, and could now analyze their doctrine with the eye of a former opponent.

I asked him why he trusted me with this. He said that Admiral Jellicoe—the original, the man whose decisions at Jutland he studies obsessively—understood that enemies often see your weaknesses more clearly than allies. The German fleet at Jutland knew exactly what the Grand Fleet could not do. This knowledge, properly used, becomes insight rather than advantage.

I am still uncertain whether I believe him. Trust does not come easily to someone who defected. But Jellicoe's approach to these documents is genuine. He cares about preservation, about accuracy, about respecting the men who wrote these reports. I can work with someone who cares about accuracy.

S-13 operated in conditions I know intimately. The cold does things to machinery, to men, to judgment. Reading these reports, I recognize the discipline required to keep an obsolete boat operational in Alaskan waters. The American captain does not complain. He notes the problems and the solutions. This is professionalism I understand across any national boundary.

—Ivan AI, Snakewater, Montana

www.ingramcontent.com/pod-product-compliance
Lightning Source LLC
LaVergne TN
LVHW061254100826
845148LV00008B/1121
9781608884513